Yorkshire

Yorkshire

Clive Hardy

Waterton Press Limited

First published in the United Kingdom in 1998 by
Frith Publishing an imprint of Waterton Press Limited.

Text and Design Copyright © Waterton Press Limited

Photographs Copyright © The Francis Frith Collection.

British Library Cataloguing in Publication Data.

Clive Hardy
Yorkshire

ISBN 1-84125-025-2

Reproductions of all the photographs in this book are available as framed or mounted prints. For more information please contact The Francis Frith Collection at the address below quoting the title of this book and the page number and photograph number or title.

The Francis Frith Collection,
PO Box 1697, Salisbury, Wilts SP3 5TW
Tel: 01747 855 669
E mail: bookprints@francisfrith.com

Typeset in Bembo Semi Bold

Printed and bound in Great Britain by
WBC Limited, Bridgend, Glamorgan.

Contents

Francis Frith 1822–1898

Introduction

Francis Frith:
A Victorian Pioneer

Francis Frith, the founder of the world famous photographic archive was a complex and multi-tudinous man. A devout Quaker and a highly successful and respected Victorian businessman he was also a flamboyant character.

By 1855 Frith had already established a wholesale grocery business in Liverpool and sold it for the astonishing sum of £200,000, equivalent of over £15,000,000 today. Now a multi-millionaire he was able to indulge in his irresistible desire to travel. As a child he had poured over books penned by early explorers, and his imagination had been stirred by family holidays to the sublime mountain regions of Wales and Scotland. "What a land of spirit-stirring and enriching scenes and places!" he had written. He was to return to these scenes of grandeur in later years to "recapture the thousands of vivid and tender memories", but with a very different purpose. Now in his thirties, and captivated by the new science of photography, Frith set out on a series of pioneering journeys to the Middle East, that occupied him from 1856 until 1860.

He took with him a specially-designed wicker carriage which acted as camera, dark-room and sleeping chamber. These far-flung journeys were full of intrigue and adventure. In his life story, written when he was sixty-three, Frith tells of being held captive by bandits, and fighting "an awful midnight battle to the very point of exhaustion and surrender with a deadly pack of hungry, wild dogs". He bargained for several weeks with a "mysterious priest" over a beautiful seven-volume illuminated Koran, which is now in the British Museum. Wearing full arab costume, Frith arrived at Akaba by camel seventy years before Lawrence of Arabia, where he encountered "desert princes and rival sheikhs, blazing with jewel-hilted swords".

During these extraordinary adventures he was assiduously exploring the desert regions of the nile and recording the antiquities and people with his camera, Frith was the first photographer ever to travel beyond the sixth cataract. Africa, we must remember, was still the "Dark Continent", and Stanley and Livingstone's famous meeting was a decade into the future. The conditions for picture taking confound belief. He laboured for hours on end in his dark-room in the sweltering heat, while the volatile collodion chemicals fizzed dangerously in their trays. Often he was forced to work in tombs and caves where conditions were cooler.

Back in London he exhibited his photographs and was "rapturously cheered" by the Royal Society. His reputation as a photographer was made overnight. His photographs were issued in albums by James S. Virtue and William MacKenzie, and published simultaneously in London and New York. An eminent historian has likened their impact on the population of the time to that on our own generation of the first photographs taken on the surface of the moon.

Characteristically, Frith spotted the potential to create a new business as a specialist publisher of photographs. In 1860 he married Mary Ann Rosling and set out to photograph every city, town and village in Britain. For the next thirty years Frith travelled the country by train and by pony and trap, producing photographs that were keenly bought by the millions of Victorians who, because of the burgeoning rail network, were beginning to enjoy holidays and day trips to Britain's seaside resorts and beauty spots.

To meet the demand he gathered together a team of up to twelve photographers, and also published the work of independent artist-photographers of the reputation of Roger Fenton and Francis Bedford. Together with clerks and photographic printers he employed a substantial staff at his Reigate studios. To gain an understanding of the scale of Frith's business one only has to look at the catalogue issued by Frith & Co. in 1886. It runs to some 670 pages listing not only many thousands of views of the British Isles but also photographs of most major European countries, and China, Japan, the USA and Canada. By 1890 Frith had created the greatest specialist photographic publishing company in the world.

He died in 1898 at his villa in Cannes, his great project still growing. His sons, Eustace and Cyril, took over the task, and Frith & Co. continued in business for another seventy years, until by 1970 the archive contained over a third of a million pictures of 7,000 cities, towns and villages.

The photographic record he has left to us stands as a living monument to a remarkable and very special man.

Frith's dhow in Egypt *c*.1857

SHEFFIELD AND THE SOUTH
Sheffield

Famous since the fourteenth century for cutlery, it was Benjamin Huntsman's discovery that steel could be purified by using a crucible, that led to Sheffield becoming the steel capital of Britain. Forges, metal working shops and steelworks came in all shapes and sizes, from those employing just a handful of men to the industrial giants like Firth Brown and Hadfields. There were other industries such as the Yorkshire Engine Co. which built railway locomotives and there were also several collieries within easy reach of the city centre. Badly damaged during the Second World War, much of the city centre was rebuilt and little now survives of the pre-Victorian era save for parts of the cathedral and a handful of houses.

PICSI08001   The canal basin in 1870, with several barges loaded with scrap metal enroute for reprocessing. The canal came right into the heart of the city close to the Corn Exchange.

PICS108006   A tramcar trundles along Fargate in 1955. On the right is the Albany Hotel and the Yorkshire Penny Bank. Sheffield was just one of a handful of authorities at this date, who still had faith in their tramway system. As late as 1948, the city was given a £200,000 loan from the Ministry of Transport to build 35 new trams.

PICS108055   Barkers Pool in 1955. On the right is the Gaumont, a classic example of the super cinema of the 1930s. In those days many people went to the cinema at least once a week. These super cinemas were designed to take your mind of the drudgery of everyday life, so for three or four hours you could leave your worries behind and enter the world of make believe.

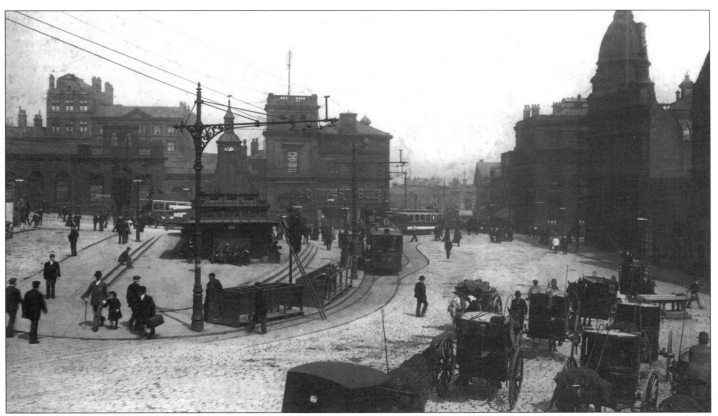

PIC48268   A busy Fitzalan Square in 1902. Electric street tramcars had been introduced in 1899 and in this picture we have a selection of single-deck and open-top double-deckers. The Corporation had taken over the tramway system in 1896, when the lease of the previous company terminated and lost no time in converting it from horse to electric traction. The single-deck trams were used on routes with low railway bridges. Note also the wooden stalls used as tramway stops.

PIC31976   Endcliffe Woods in 1893. This park was laid out for the benefit of working people to give them a break from the dust and grime of industrial Sheffield.

PICB335014   Four miles south of Sheffield are the ruins of Beauchief Abbey. Founded in 1175, all that now remains is the west tower.

Doncaster

Doncaster is another one of those towns like Derby which owes its transformation from an agricultural to an industrial centre, to the coming of the railways. Authorised to build a line from Askern to London by way of Retford, Lincoln, Boston and Peterborough, the Great Northern Railway chose Doncaster for the site of its locomotive and carriage and wagon workshops. Coal mining was also a major employer, Doncaster being ringed with pit villages. Shafts continued to be sunk well into the twentieth century. The first sod was cut at Brodsworth Colliery in 1905 and at Hatfield Main in 1911. At Hatfield it took five years to reach the Barnsley bed at 852 yards below the surface.

PIC49857   Humber keel boats on the river in 1903. In the background is the great parish church of St George's built in 1858 to replace an earlier one which had been destroyed by fire five years earlier. The story goes that as the old church went up in flames, the vicar exclaimed, "Good gracious, and I have left my false teeth in the vestry!"

PIC35313   The High Street in 1895. Along here could be found the imposing edifice of the York City & County Bank, the Yorkshire Penny Bank and the eighteenth century Reindeer Hotel. In 1909, the Danum Hotel was built to the left of where the cameraman stood to take this picture.

PIC49853   Baxtergate at the junction of St Sepulchre Gate and the High Street in 1903. It was down Baxtergate that Freeman, Hardy and Willis had their branch and where those who had signed the pledge could find a room at the Albany Temperance Hotel.

PIC35317A   Set on a Knoll overlooking the River Don stands Conisbrough Castle. Built out of the local creamy-white limestone the keep is 90 ft high and has six semi-hexagonal buttresses, which rise above it to form mini-turrets. When Sir Walter Scott visited Conisbrough, he was so impressed with the tiny chapel set into one of the buttresses that he included it in his novel *Ivanhoe*. This picture was taken in 1895.

BRADFORD & INDUSTRIAL
WEST YORKSHIRE
Bradford

Without doubt Bradford was the centre of the woollen and worsted industry, not only in this country but throughout the world. The Victorian traveller would have found the city skyline a veritable forest of mill chimneys, but there were other industries. Bradford was on the western edge of the great Yorkshire coalfield, and because the coal was near to the surface, it could be mined relatively inexpensively. Also close by were the ironworks of Bowling and Low Moor.

PIC39509   Market Street in 1897. In the background is the Venetian Gothic-style Wool Exchange, which was said to present an animated sight on Mondays and Thursdays when the traders did their buying and selling.

PIC49713   Trams stop to pick up passengers in Tyrell Street in 1903. Electric street tramcars were introduced in the city from 1898 and ran until 1950.

PIC49712   On the right is the Town Hall in all its Gothic splendour which was completed in 1873 at a cost of £100,000.

PIC39506   Forster Square in 1897. On the right is a statue of Richard Oastler, who fought against the use of child labour in the mills. The large building in the background is the Post Office which was open from seven in the morning till ten at night.

B173028   Victoria Square just a few months before the abandonment of the tramway system in 1950. In the background a trolleybus is about to pass a tram as it heads towards the Town Hall. The trolleybus was developed on the Continent. Like the electric tramcar, it drew current from an overhead power supply but did not require rails to run on. On 20 June 1911, a joint scheme between Leeds and Bradford saw the inauguration of the first trolleybus service in Great Britain. Bradford would also be the last city in Britain to operate trolleybuses.

PIC49711   Forster Square in 1903. Named after the Bradford MP, W. E. Forster, who sponsored the compulsory education act of 1870. It was due to people like Forster, that Bradford was the first to have school medical services, school meals, a school board, school baths and nursery provision. Lurking behind the post office is the parish church; it became a cathedral in 1919.

PIC74400   Lister Park in 1921. The park is named after Lord Masham and includes a boating lake, a scented garden for the blind and the Cartwright Memorial Hall which was opened in 1904.

Halifax

Set in the foothills of the Pennines, Halifax is one of the great cloth towns of England and has been a producer of cloth since the thirteenth century. The Piece Hall completed in 1779 was where wool merchants traded and weavers sold their pieces. This superb building still stands. It has 315 rooms on three stories around a quadrangle. Halifax is also where English toffee was invented, and it was here in 1934 that Percy Shaw produced the first cats' eyes, or to give them their proper name, reflecting road studs.

PICH9001   The Town Hall was designed in the Italian style by Sir Charles Barry and built in 1863 and is famous for its extraordinary looking clock tower. In this picture taken in 1900, the Town Hall can be seen in the background. Note also the rough pavement setts and the juddering cobbled road. On the left is a boy selling milk from the churn.

PIC38778   A busy scene in Crown Street in 1896. On the left we have Smith's umbrella shop, which had just diversified into wedding and birthday presents.

PIC38777   This is the entrance to the Market Hall as it looked in 1896. Inside, stalls were laid out in regular rows, with clothing, material and footwear stalls to the middle and foodstuffs to the outside.

PICH9068 A general view of Halifax dating from 1965. St John's, which is the old parish church dating from the twelfth century, is on the right-hand side almost surrounded by warehouses, factories and the railway.

PIC38781 This photograph taken in 1896 of looms and other equipment installed in a workshop in the local technical school, reinforces the importance of the cloth industry to the town. In fact it was so important that Halifax had been granted its own laws for dealing with people convicted of stealing cloth. The law was limited to the forest of Hardwick, including the eighteen towns and villages within its boundary. 'That if a felon be taken within the liberty of the forest of Hardwick, with goods stolen out or within said precincts, either hand-habend, backberand or confessioned, to the value of thirteen pence halfpenny, he shall, after three market-days within the town of Halifax, next after such apprehension and being condemned, be taken to the gibbet and there have his head cut from his body.' Halifax had a decapitating machine; Dr Guillotine simply built and improved on the idea.

PIC38782   A good view of the inside of the Market Hall. The glass roof is supported on ornamental columns made of cast-iron. The market appears light and airy and there seems to be plenty of space around the stalls.

PICH9098   The Odeon Cinema, Broad Street, in 1965 faces yet another competitor for peoples leisure time. The 1960s was the period when the film studios were turning out some great motion pictures, but audiences were falling due to the popularity of television, bingo and more people becoming car owners. The new threat here is from a bowling alley. Ten pin bowling was imported from the USA, with many towns opening state-of-the-art alleys. However, in many areas the craze lasted only a few years and a large number of alleys subsequently closed down.

PICH9070   The railway cuts a swathe through Halifax, yet given the town's importance, there was a sense of outrage when the Manchester & Leeds Railway bypassed the town with no connecting branch line built. A branch line was promised as early as 1841, but until July 1844 the only way manufacturers could get their products to a rail-head was by horse and cart to Elland station.

Haworth

Haworth is about the same size today as it was in the mid-nineteenth century with a population of about 6,500. Being just ten miles from Halifax and twelve miles from Bradford, this grim hard-featured town of grey-stone houses became a place for textile factories. Many visitors find it hard to believe that Haworth is also a literary shrine capable of giving Stratford-upon-Avon a run for its money. It was at Haworth parsonage that the three Bronte sisters, Charlotte, Emily and Anne lived and worked.

H194052   A general view of Haworth taken in 1955. Mr Bronte was the vicar of St Michael and All Angels. The church is still there, but the Brontes would only recognise the west tower, the remainder having been demolished and rebuilt in 1880.

Bingley

Set in the valley of the River Aire, Bingley was once the classical picture of a nineteenth century worsted-weaving and textile town, with its great mills and tall smokestacks.

PIC34755   This is the old Market House in 1894. Note the stocks situated to the left of the base of the market cross.

PIC74416   Boating on the Aire in 1923. Over on the far side of the river, behind the brick wall is part of the gasworks. When this picture was taken, the Aire had already been polluted for several decades, as mills discharged waste directly into it.

PIC34748   Five-Rise Locks on the Leeds and Liverpool Canal in 1894. The locks lifted boats and barges a full 60 ft, and is one of the most impressive groups of locks on the canal. The canal was a vital link for Bingley's manufacturers with the port of Liverpool.

PIC61871   Saltaire station on the Midland Railway main line from Bradford to Skipton in 1909. Saltaire owes its existence to Sir Titus Salt, who moved his alpaca and mohair mills here in the 1850s. Sir Titus was convinced that his workers would have a healthier environment to live and work in.

PIC61872   Apart from the ladies with the perambulator, Saltaire Park appears to be deserted in this picture from 1909. It might have been a requirement that the Frith cameraman take the picture with as few people as possible on it. This was often done at this time, purely for commercial and not artistic reasons.

Leeds

The industrial power house of the old West Riding. There was an enormous variety to the manufacturing base of the city including, railway locomotives from the Hunslet Engine Co., Manning Wardle & Co., Kitsons, and Hudswell Clarke. John Fowler & Co. built roadrollers, traction engines and farm machinery, and there were a number of companies producing castings of various sorts. There were bleaching works, flax mills, leather factories and chemical plants. Leeds also became the leading centre for the manufacture of ready-to-wear clothes.

PIC39088   Leeds post office and Revenue Office in 1897. The postal service in Victorian times was considered a vital part of the public good with offices in major cities having long opening hours.

PIC28281   The parish church of St Peter in Kirkgate in 1891. There are no medieval churches in central Leeds, though several date from the seventeenth and eighteenth centuries.

PIC34767   The red-brick Yorkshire College as it looked in 1894. It was out of this college that Leeds university was established in 1904. Leeds Mechanics' Institute was also noted for its high standards. Members of the Institute were also adventurous, hiring Thomas Cook in June 1840 to organize a members' excursion to York by way of the Leeds & Selby and the York & North Midland Railways. The trip was priced at half the normal fare and included tea at York.

PIC39099   The home of Yorkshire CCC, this is what Headingly looked like in 1897.

PIC28286   Kirkstall Abbey played a part in the industrial development of Leeds, for it was here that iron forging first began in the district. The Abbey was founded in 1152, as a daughter house of Fountains. Building work was completed by 1175 and iron forging began in 1200. This picture was taken in 1890.

ILKLEY, SKIPTON & THE MOORS
Ilkley

Ilkley was just another one horse town until 1850, when the spring waters were declared beneficial to health and so another spa town was born. Villas, hotels and hydros sprang up, and within a few years Ilkley was claiming to be the Malvern of the North.

PIC63557   Brook Street in 1911. Carriages wait patiently on the station approach for another train load of health seekers bound for any of the seven listed hydros. Taking the treatment cost £2.5s.0d a week, though a number of guides hinted that the local bracing air had perhaps as much medicinal value as the waters.

PIC63556   The Grove in 1911. The road to the right leads to the railway station, but directly along the leafy street is The Spa, a particularly popular hydro.

PICI6006   The open air bathing pool in 1960. There was a time when most places seemed to possess an open air pool, and though popular on hot sunny days, many were in fact closed down for various health and safety reasons.

PIC67335   The moors above Ilkley. In 1914, when this picture was taken, moorland walking had still to catch on, most walkers were ill-equipped and ladies were expected to turn out in long dresses and totally inadequate footwear. One popular walk was up Heber's Gill to the Swastika Stone, an ancient area which may have been used for fire worship.

PIC18510   The ruins of Bolton Abbey are near a sweeping bend of the River Wharfe, and proved a great attraction for painters, including Landseer and Turner. The priory was founded in the twelfth century, building work continuing right up to the Dissolution. The nave survived, to be used as the parish church and during the late nineteenth century the rectory served as a free school. The picture was taken in 1886.

Skipton

A centre for sheep and cattle rearing, and situated at the edge of a wild tract of limestone country, the town was generally called Skipton-in-Craven. Its two main features are the castle, which stood a three year siege from December 1642 to December 1645, and the extensively restored Holy Trinity Church.

PIC33157   Skipton High Street on a market day, some time in 1893. In the background is the parish church which was damaged during the siege of the castle in the Civil War. It contains some elaborate monuments to the Clifford Family, and was in fact restored by Lady Anne Clifford before she died in 1675.

PIC74507   Swadford Street in 1923. By this date the motorcar and charabanc had put Skipton firmly on the map as the principal southern gateway to the Dales. The town boasted one RAC listed and two AA recommended hotels, namely The Ship, The Black Horse and The Devonshire.

PIC45779   The small cobblestoned market square at Grassington in 1900. The village had once been a centre for lead-mining but now relied on agriculture and quarrying. In 1902 the railway finally came to the Grassington with the opening of a line to Skipton.

PIC45794   On the river at Burnsall. In the background is St Wilfred's which was repaired in 1612 at the expense of Sir William Craven. The church houses an eleventh century font and some fragments of Anglo-Saxon sculpture. At the oar of the boat is a woman - quite adventurous for 1900.

PIC45769   The Upper Falls at Clapham in 1900. In 1857, Ingleborough Cave was made accessible and from that, Clapham became a centre for potholing. Nearby is Gaping Gill, which has an underground chamber large enough to house a cathedral.

PIC26330   Set amid the spectacular scenery of the River Greta and Clapham Beck, this is the village of Ingleton in 1890. Francis Frith had already set up a stockist to sell his postcards; the display board is to the left of the shop window.

PIC71339   A bustling Tuesday market in Settle in 1921. On the right is the Elizabethan-style Town Hall built in 1832. In the background smothered with drying washing are the shambles. These date from the seventeenth century and comprised several shops in an arched arcade and living accommodation above.

HARROGATE &
THE SURROUNDING AREA
Harrogate

One of the oldest and most favourite of all the English spa towns, the curative mineral springs were discovered here by Sir William Slingsby in 1571. In the 1840s the town was developed by the Duchy of Lancaster, the first public baths opening in 1842.

PIC58645   Valley Gardens in 1907 was a favourite venue for mild constitutionals after taking the waters. Here a small crowd no doubt enjoy an afternoon concert party given by a Pierrot troupe.

PIC63514   Two elegantly dressed ladies take an afternoon stroll through Crescent Gardens. In the background the crowd is gathering, and the awnings are being taken down off the bandstand. The music is about to begin.

PIC74569   The Royal Pump Room as it looked in 1923. In 1902, bumpers of sulphuric and chalybeate were dispensed here from seven o'clock in the morning onwards. After taking the first glass, a mild constitutional in Valley Gardens was recommended.

PIC39430   The Royal Baths, photographed shortly after they had opened in 1897. They were said to be unequalled in decoration and roominess and for 5/6*d* you could get a 'mud bath' with electricity. From 1949, the cure was available on the NHS.

PIC58649   Drug Wars in Parliament Street in 1907. On the right, Taylors' Drug Store boldly displays its name in six foot high gilt lettering. Not to be outdone, the chemist just across the road proclaims that his establishment is the largest in the world. Harrogate had become a fashionable town noted for its fine shops and rich teas.

PIC74585   When this picture was taken in 1923, Ripley consisted of just one street. The village was extensively remodelled in the 1820s, though parts of the parish church date from the fourteenth century. The picture shows the cobbled square, complete with stocks and the village cross. In the churchyard is what is claimed to be, the only weeping cross in the whole of Yorkshire. Around the base are eight niches in which to kneel and repent.

Ripon

Ripon is one of England's smallest cathedral cities, having been such since 1836, when it became the centre of a new bishopric. The oldest part of the cathedral is the crypt, which dates from the original seventh century church built by St Wilfred.

PIC35260   Pictured in 1895, the cathedral at Ripon looks massive, but is in fact relatively small, the central and two western towers being of no great height. The original church built by St Wilfred was destroyed in 950 AD. The present cathedral dates from the twelfth and thirteenth centuries; the west front considered to be one of the finest examples of early English work still extant.

PIC47179   Market day in Ripon in 1901. The obelisk dates from 1781 and was raised to commemorate William Aislabie, who was the local MP for sixty years.

PIC35278   The majestic ruins of Fountains Abbey as they looked in 1895. Founded in poverty in 1132 by a group of monks from St Mary's Abbey, York, Fountains eventually became very wealthy. The ruins date from the twelfth to the fifteenth centuries, the tower which was built between 1492 and 1524 being the latest part.

PIC18352   Fountains Abbey in 1886. Henry VIII sold Fountains to Sir Richard Gresham in 1540, and though some seventy years later Sir Stephen Proctor used abbey stone to build Fountains Hall, the ruins are still impressive and preserve the plan of this great monastery almost intact.

PICT306030   Market day in Thirsk in 1955. During the eighteenth and nineteenth centuries, Thirsk was one of the posting stations serving the Great North Road, The Fleece being the main coaching inn.

Boroughbridge

Boroughbridge dates back to Norman times, when a bridge was constructed over the River Ure. In 1322 the Earl of Lancaster sought refuge in the local church following his defeat by Edward II. The unfortunate earl was taken prisoner and carted off to his own castle at Pontefract, where he was beheaded.

PIC58630   Boroughbridge probably saw its best days when it was a coaching town for traffic on the Great North Road, and had no less than twenty-two inns. This picture shows the 14 bedroom, Three Greyhounds Hotel as it looked in 1907.

PIC58636   Aldborough, just one mile from Boroughbridge, stands on the site of the Roman station, Isurium and has a museum containing Roman remains. In this picture taken in 1907, children play round the old stone cross, said to commemorate the Battle of Boroughbridge. The carter has stopped to let the cameraman take the picture. Note that the girls all appear to be wearing smocks and hats.

PIC58637   The maypole at Aldborough. Used in a ritual folk dance, the pole was decorated with flowers and coloured ribbons that were woven into intricate patterns as the dancers did their stuff. It is thought that the pole was a substitute for the living tree used in earlier fertility rites.

Knaresborough

The ancient market town of Knaresborough clings to the limestone bluff of a gorge carved by the River Nidd. The town is famous for several things: the oldest woollen mill in England, Mother Shipton, a fifteenth century prophetess who allegedly forecast motorcars, aircraft and so on, and Blind Jack Metcalf, who was born in 1717 and during 93 years of hell raising, was a soldier, roadbuilder, forest guide and musician.

PIC71687   Knaresborough on a bustling market day in 1921.

PIC20946　　　　Knaresborough in 1888. The church on the left is St John's, the tower of which is topped off with a small spirelet and dates from the thirteenth and fourteenth centuries. In 1318, a Scottish raiding party attempted to destroy the tower and the people who had taken shelter there, by setting it alight. The Scots failed, but for centuries afterwards traces of the burning could still be seen.

PIC63532　　　　A view of the river in 1911. Moored alongside the far bank is a floating tea rooms which appears to be doing a brisk trade. The rowing boat in the foreground is in fact the ferry to the Dropping Well. On the hill above the town stands the ruins of Knaresborough Castle, which was destroyed by Parliament in 1648.

PIC67264   The Dropping Well in 1914. This is a petrifying well, similar to the one at Matlock Bath in Derbyshire, where the limestone content of the spring water solidifies objects which fall into it. At one time there was a petrified mongoose on exhibition, mind you it was in Yorkshire. . . .

PIC55009   Knaresborough Castle in 1906. A Norman castle had been built here by Baron Serlo de Burg but the ruins date from the fourteenth century. During the reign of King John, the castle was a royal arsenal, manufacturing 109,000 crossbow quarrels. In the early years of Edward II's reign, Knaresborough was extensively rebuilt due to the lordship having been given to the king's favourite, Piers Gaveston. It was also here that Richard II was imprisoned, prior to being taken to Pontefract where he was murdered.

PIC61730 The High Street, Wetherby in 1909. The Angel Hotel on the left, was one of three to cater for the motorist, the others being the George and Dragon, and the Brunswick. Wetherby had been an important stopover during the days of the stagecoach, but since the coming of the railways has had to rely more and more on tourists.

PIC61731 North Street in 1909. Ward & Sons were established in 1868, and had probably been smiths and/or farriers, until deciding to concentrate on vehicle repairs and the selling of bicycles. As can be seen from the picture, they were also the local AA agents. Further down the street Continental Motors are the local Michelin agents.

PIC61729   This is Wetherby Market Place in 1909. At the turn of the century it was described as 'a town with no interest'. In 1920 the Dunlop Guide added 'pleasant walks along the river'.

Boston Spa

In 1744 a man by the name of John Shires discovered a saline spring, and given the eighteenth century fashion for taking the waters Boston Spa was born.

PIC32000　　　Like most spas, Boston had its moment of glory, and for a few years was the place to be seen. A stagecoach service was operated on a daily basis from Leeds and back, and wealthy travellers using the Great North Road would stop over and sample the delights of the pump room.

PIC39445   This is Clifford village, just one mile from Boston Spa and even less from the Great North Road. One of the interesting things when looking at some of these photographs, is the number of shops that even the smallest of villages seemed to have. Nowadays, because we are all bone idle and have been sucked in to thinking convenience shopping is something wonderful, village shops, post offices, and even pubs are in decline.

THE YORKSHIRE COAST FROM HULL TO STAITHES
Hull

Hull, the third largest port in Britain, still has docks running for several miles along the north bank of the Humber, handling hundreds of millions of pounds worth of cargo and thousands of passengers every year. And despite savage reductions in the fishing fleet and EU quoter system, it remains one of our principal fishing ports, though much of the fish is either landed from foreign trawlers or arrives by lorry from other UK ports. The pictures from the Frith collection were mostly taken at the turn of the twentieth century, when Hull made its living almost exclusively from the sea and shipbuilding. The pictures are also of interest, because Hull was virtually rebuilt after the Second World War, having been hardest hit of all the northern ports.

PIC49809   Hull Market Place in 1903. To the right is the Cross Keys Hotel, but the most famous of all is Ye Old White Harte Inn, where the Governor and other leading citizens of Hull took the decision not to let King Charles I enter the city in 1642.

PIC49813
The Market Place in 1903. The ancient parish church of Holy Trinity dates from the thirteenth to fifteenth centuries and has an unusual brick-built chancel.

PIC49814   An open-top tramcar in George Street in 1903. Electric trams had been introduced to the city in 1899. On 30 June 1945, Hull became the first city in the country to abandon its tramway since the outbreak of the Second World War. Many of the trams were sold to the Leeds Corporation.

PIC49807   The imposing Dock Offices reinforces Hull's position as a major port. The Doric column on the right is a monument to William Wilberforce, who was born in Hull, and was responsible for the abolition of slavery throughout the Empire.

PIC49820   A busy scene on the Humber in 1903. As well as general cargo shipped through the port, the amount of fish landed at St Andrew's Dock during that year, amounted to 1,580,959 cwts.

Bridlington

Bridlington lies near the top of Bridlington Bay, its northern flank protected by the great headland of Flamborough some six miles distant. The old town is in fact one mile inland from the sea, where in 1119, Walter de Grant founded an Augustine priory. On 22 February 1643, Queen Henrietta Maria landed at Bridlington with much needed arms and ammunition for King Charles. Bombarded by warships of the Parliamentary navy, the Queen took shelter until it was considered safe to move on to Boynton Hall.

PIC39371   Princess Street, Bridlington in 1897. One of the principal shopping streets for this town of around 13,000 people. During the holiday season, the town's population could easily double. Bridlington was within easy reach of trippers from Hull, Leeds, Beverley and York.

PIC55752   A good general view of Princess Parade in 1906, showing some of the well laid out flower beds that Bridlington had a reputation for producing.

Filey

Situated eleven miles north of Bridlington, Filey was for many years, a working fishing village, but became a popular place in the 1890s for those seeking a quiet holiday away from already developed resorts such as Scarborough. An ideal place for children, Filey was noted for its very fine sands and rugged scenery. The southern horn of the bay is dominated by the spectacular height of Flamborough Head, whilst the northern horn is formed by the mile-long low reef known as Filey Brigg. It was off Flamborough Head during the American War of Independence, that the USS *Bonhomme Richard* commanded by John Paul Jones, defeated the more heavily armed HMS *Serapis*.

PIC48020A   Looking south toward Flamborough Head in 1901. Deckchairs and beach tents were available for hire, and the donkeys are saddled to take different age groups. The harp and the clown-like costumes are in fact the tell-tale signs that a Pierrot seaside concert party is touting for customers. Pierrot were in vogue right upto the Second World War, and their origins go back to the London success of the mime play *L'Enfant Prodigue* staged in 1891.

PIC39343   The Promenade in 1897. On the right, Archibald Ramsden's bathing machines offered discreet changing facilities for those wishing to take an invigorating plunge into the bay. The small horse-drawn carts carried less active holiday makers onto the sands, but could probably be hired as an alternative to a donkey ride.

PIC48018   Promenade in 1901. The Pierrot are getting in a late afternoon performance, whilst several holiday makers take a pre-dinner stroll. As with several other views, the photographer is facing toward the northern horn of the bay, Filey Brigg being a popular haunt of amateur geologists and fossil hunters.

Scarborough

At just under 21 miles from Whitby, Scarborough rapidly developed to become the premier resort of the Yorkshire coast, and was often overrun with day trippers like Blackpool. But there was a difference between them. Scarborough had two seasons: a fashionable one and a popular one. An ancient town as well as a seaport, Scarborough takes its name from the cliffs or scars on which William of Aumale, Earl of Yorkshire built a castle in the twelfth century. Later a royal fortress, Scarborough endured two determined sieges in 1645 and 1648, on both occasions the garrison surrendered to the Roundheads. War came to the town once more in December 1914 when it was shelled by units of the German High Seas Fleet.

PIC28817   This is Westborough in 1891. One of the main thoroughfares linking the North Eastern Railway station and the town. On the right is Winebloom's Railway Hotel and Robinson's Cash Boot Stores, whilst over on the left is Graham's Adelphi Commercial Hotel.

PIC23476   Belmont, possibly during the fashionable season in 1890. Here a group of people take the chance to admire the view over Spa Cliffs, or catch up with the latest news. The Spa by this time was long gone, having been destroyed by fire in 1876. In its place an exotic Turkish style pavilion was built containing a concert hall, art gallery, theatre and restaurant.

PIC23453   Spa Promenade in 1890 was one of the main attractions. On the beach in the background are a number of bathing machines, not unlike caravans but smaller. The machine would have a door and a pair of shafts at either end. The lady wishing to bathe would enter the machine from the landward side, whilst a horse would be attached to the seaward end. Once inside, the lady would put on her bathing apparel and the machine would then be pulled into the water. The lady would then emerge through the front door and slip, dignity intact, into the sea. Whilst the lady was bathing, the horse would be harnessed to the other end of the machine for the return journey.

PIC23459   The South Cliff Tramway offered holiday makers an alternative means of escape from the beach to the Esplanade, other than by the 224 steps cutting through the Spa Gardens, and all for just 1*d*.

PIC28812   Scarborough Castle dominates this 1891 picture of Foreshore Road. Once standing 100 ft tall, with walls 12 ft thick, the keep was positioned in such a way so as to command the approach to the causeway leading to the castle. Any attacking force attempting to enter the bailey, would first of all have to run the gauntlet of defending fire from the keep's battlements.

PIC23464   Another view of Foreshore Road facing away from the castle. In the foreground is a market where trippers could buy fresh fish off the local boats. On the right, is the lifeboat station. The lifeboat was slung on a wheeled cradle which would be hauled out of the station, down the ramp immediately in front of it and into the sea; the boat floating off once there was sufficient water under her.

PIC23471   Lying alongside Vincents Pier in 1890, the paddle steamer *Comet* loads up with passengers for an excursion trip round the headland. These small steamers were a feature of both the Scarborough and Bridlington holiday trade which survived until they were replaced by screw vessels in the 1930s.

PIC23466   A Lowestoft registered fishing boat slips out to sea unnoticed by the anglers on the harbour. In the background, is the imposing, if somewhat overpowering edifice of the Grand Hotel. By 1920 Scarborough could boast no less than ten top hotels including the 100 bedroom Pavilion and the 160 bedroom Manor Private. The telephone number for the Grand was Scarborough 11.

Robin Hood's Bay

The fishing village of Robin Hood's Bay lies just a few miles to the south of Whitby. Also known as Bay Town, it became a favourite haunt for artists and holidaymakers alike. The connection with the legend of Robin Hood is obscure, but one story is that Robin came here to hire boats in order to escape from England.

PIC80183   As can be seen here in this picture taken in 1928, part of the village is clustered around the top of a ravine; notice the steep flight of steps in the lower foreground dropping away down toward the sea. In the background, the bay sweeps round to Ravenscar, the 'town that never was.' Apparently there were plans to turn Ravenscar into another Scarborough, but the scheme failed due to the unstable geology of the area.

PIC80187   For decades, just as in this picture from 1927, people have sunned themselves along the sea wall.
The Bay Hotel is on the right.

PIC80185   Exploring rock pools back in 1927. One of the reasons why Robin Hood's Bay proved to be a popular haunt for artists, is the cluster of red-roofed cottages perched somewhat precariously on the cliffs. Over the last 200 years or so, erosion has only managed to claim two rows of houses and a road.

Whitby

Situated in a deep ravine on the estuary of the river Esk, Whitby earned its living from the sea, either by whaling, fishing, coastal trading or shipbuilding. For centuries it was often easier for people coming to, or going from Whitby, to make their journey by sea rather than attempt to travel overland. The coming of the railway changed all that. Whitby was now firmly on the map, its narrow crowded alleys and harbourside streets, a ruined abbey and souvenirs made from jet, fossilised wood found in the local area, proved a magnet for day trippers and holiday makers. The holiday trade led to the development of the town, chiefly in the direction of the West Cliff, where hotels and guest houses were built. But Whitby is an ancient town. It was here in the seventh century that St Hilda founded what would become one of the most famous monasteries of the Celtic world. Here worked Caedmon, the first recorded English Christian poet. It was also here in AD 667 that the Synod of Whitby settled the differences between the Celtic and the Roman methods of determining the dates for Easter.

PIC46790   The extensive ruins of Whitby Abbey photographed in 1901. The ruins are not those of the Abbey Church built by St Hilda, but of the one that replaced it in the thirteenth century. Adjacent to the Abbey is the old Whitby parish church of St Mary's, which is reached from the harbour by a flight of 199 steps known locally as 'Jacob's Ladder'. St Mary's was made famous in Bram Stoker's Gothic novel *Dracula*, for it was here that the count sought refuge in the grave of a suicide.

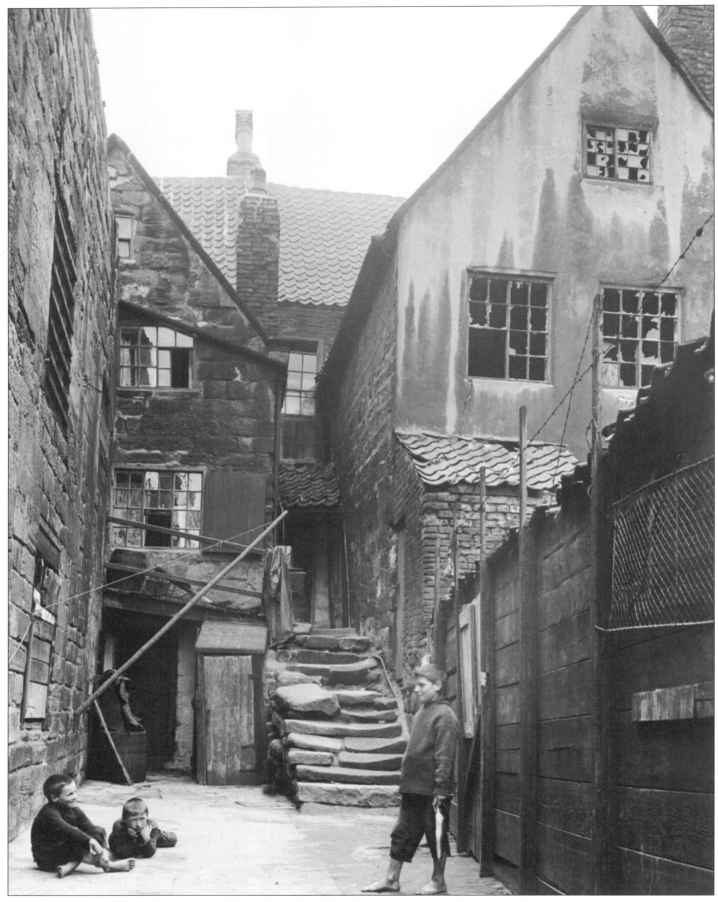

PIC66290   This is Arguments Yard in 1913. The house on the right is derelict, the stone stairs have seen better days and the outside toilet looks ready to collapse at any minute.

PIC66266   The bridge was a favourite place where people could stop for a chat, or simply stand and watch the world go by. The small hut is the control point for the bridge which could be raised to allow shipping through.

PIC18167   A fine view looking down St Anne's Staith.

PIC74309   A bustling if somewhat winding Baxtergate in 1923. In the centre of town, it contained the post office, The Angel Hotel (telephone number Whitby 57) and St John's Church as well as many shops. By this time Whitby could boast no less than five hotels in the Dunlop Motorist's Guide, The Angel, The Royal (with 172 bedrooms and garage parking for 20 cars), The Metropole, The Custom House and the 70 bedroom West Cliff.

PIC78993   Sandsend was just three miles along the sandy beach from Whitby. A popular place for holidays when this picture was taken in 1925, even though the village was disfigured by a ruin of an alum works and an iron bridge carrying the LNER railway line from Whitby to Saltburn. To the north lies the Kettleness, or rather what's left of it. During a violent storm in 1829, the cliff fell into the sea taking most of Kettleness with it.

PIC18202   The fishing village of Runswick Bay is set on a sheer cliff. It is also one of the most attractive harbourless villages along the Yorkshire coast. When this picture was taken in 1886, fishermen would have to wait for high tide before launching their boats from the beach.

PIC80194   Runswick Bay in 1927. Even when not fishing, there was always work to be done, repairing nets and maintaining the boats. Perhaps the fisherman is yarning to the kids about the hob (Yorkshire goblin), said to live in the hollows to the south of the village. The hob was fond of children and said to be able to cure ailments.

Staithes

During the nineteenth and early twentieth centuries, Staithes was a fishing port of some standing, being a centre for cod, haddock and mackerel, but fell into decline with the development of steam trawlers which tended to be concentrated on the larger ports of Hull, Grimsby, Bridlington, Scarborough and Whitby. At one time the North Eastern Railway ran three or four special fish trains a week out of Staithes.

PIC79004   As with several other fishing villages along the Yorkshire coast, Staithes clings alpine like to the sides of steep cliffs and ravines. This picture was taken in 1925, and though the old gentleman could well be delivering fresh milk, yolks were used for carrying all sorts of things up the steep streets.

PICS176001   This picture dates back to around 1890, and shows a group busy baiting lines. Lining was one of the principal methods of catching fish. These are fairly small lines for use by local fishermen, trawlers however, would tow a line perhaps half a mile or more in length, which with branches could have as many as 15,000 hooks.

PIC18208   Staithes in 1886. The village is said to have begun as a result of a shipwreck, when the survivors from a French ship scrambled ashore and decided to stay. As with Robin Hood's Bay, smuggling was a way of life here in the eighteenth century.

SWALEDALE

To the north of Wensleydale, Swaledale's main industry during the eighteenth and nineteenth centuries was lead mining. One of the principal centres was at Reeth, the largest community in Swaledale apart from Richmond, which by 1823 had a population of over 1400. By the 1880s, competition from overseas suppliers sounded the death knell for the lead mining industry and Swaledale reverted to farming.

PIC38295   The village of Muker toward the western end of the dale dates back to 1274. After a chapel of ease was built here in 1580, the delightfully named Corpse Way gradually fell into disuse. Until then, the bodies of people from Upper Swaledale had to be carried all the way to Grinton Church for Christian burial. Along the route there were coffin stones, on which the coffin was placed whilst the bearers got their breath back. Apparently one of these stones still exists and can be seen on the north side of Ivelet Bridge.

Richmond

The town of Richmond grew up round the Norman castle, which was begun around the year 1071 by Alan Rufus, a son of the Duke of Brittany, and William the Conqueror's man in these parts. By the time the castle was finished some two centuries later, Richmond had grown in size and a market was held here in 1155. By 1440 the town was trading in dairy produce, wine, fish, garlic, silk, iron, coal, copper and lead.

PIC74350   The castle and bridge in 1923. The Norman fortress, begun by Alan Rufus dominates the entrance to Swaledale. When the castle was begun, the border between that part of England firmly under Norman control and those still willing to put up a fight, lay just a few miles to the north.

PIC59492   Richmond Market Place in 1908. In the background is Holy Trinity Church, a most unusual building, which in the 1900s include a tobacconists, a bank, and two butchers shops as component parts of the building. It now houses the regimental museum of The Green Howards.

PIC59493   A steep lane climbs up round the edge of the castle. This picture was taken in 1909 and gives us an idea of the impressive appearance of the twelfth century keep. Richmond is one of those castles where the keep is positioned at or near the gate, which suggests that it was intended for an offensive, rather than defensive role. It also contains Scollard's Hall, built in 1080 and probably the oldest domestic building in Britain.

PIC32290   The remains of the Premonstratensian Abbey of St Agatha at Easby. The abbey was founded in 1155 by the Constable of Richmond Castle, the members of the Order were known as the White Canons after the colour of their habits.

PIC66034   Close to what would become Catterick Camp, Hipswell Hall had seen better days than when this picture was taken in 1913. When the camp was built, it took in Scotton Hall, the Hipswell estate and the Brough estate.

PIC65487   Catterick village in 1913. It was at Catterick in AD 625 that Paulinus, first Bishop of York, baptised converts to Christianity, following the marriage of King Edwin of Northumbria to Ethelburga of Kent. Catterick is the site of the Roman city of Catteractonium.

WENSLEYDALE
Hawes

Granted a market charter by William III, Hawes later became a centre for textiles, quarrying and the production of Wensleydale cheese. The town's growth was helped with the coming of the railways, Hawes being jointly operated by the Midland and the North Eastern. Cheese production had been farmhouse-based, but towards the end of the last century a factory was built. The original recipe used by the monks of Jervaulx, used the milk from ewe's, however, later farmhouse and factory cheese used milk from shorthorn cows.

PIC45635   The village school in 1900. Behind and to the right is the turreted tower of the parish church. Built in 1851, it replaced the original church dating from the reign of Richard III.

Bainbridge

Bainbridge was once an important junction, for here the roads to and from Lancaster, Swaledale and Westmorland met. In Roman times a fort stood on nearby Brough Hill, and a garrison was maintained here from about AD 80 to around the end of the fourth century.

PIC75709   Bainbridge village in 1924. The old arched bridge crosses the Bain, which at just miles in length is reputed to be the shortest river in England.

PIC56025　　The Green in 1906. It is believed that Bainbridge was a settlement for woodsmen working in the great forest of Wensleydale. An annual custom associated with this tradition, is the blowing of a forest horn every night from the end of September to Shrovetide.

PIC67235　　Farm workers at Addleborough in 1914. Addleborough peak is in the background and is believed to be named after a British chieftain, Authulf.

Askrigg

Askrigg is a small market town with a long history, and was already prosperous when the Domesday book was compiled. Askrigg continued as the leading commercial and industrial centre of Upper Wensleydale until 1699, when Hawes was granted a market charter. From then onwards Askrigg fell into decline. Local industry included brewing, spinning, dyeing, cotton and worsted manufacture and lead mining.

PIC63468   The old market cross in 1911. Many of the people who worked in the mills or mines lived in dilapidated cottages hidden behind the imposing three-storey buildings on the main street.

PIC67231   The parish church and the King's Arms Hotel in 1914. One of Askrigg's main industries was clockmaking, and it is said that more timepieces were made here than anywhere else in the North Riding.

PIC60790   This is a view of Aysgarth in 1911. Lying about ten miles east of Hawes, Aysgarth is famous for a series of waterfalls on the River Ure, the upper of which can still be viewed from a sixteenth century single-arch bridge. The village became popular with visitors to the falls.

PIC63473   The tiny village of Castle Bolton in 1911. In the background are the ruins of Bolton Castle, which was built by Richard Scrope in the 1380s. Though designed as a fortress, the castles principal function appears to have been residential; it was one of the first to have chimneys. Mary Queen of Scots was imprisoned here for six months and the castle was partially dismantled at the end of the Civil War. The castle was then used by local families who lived in tenements built within the walls, the last of these leaving in 1898.

Leyburn

Once nothing more than a tiny hamlet in the parish of Wensley, Leyburn developed into a market town thanks to a charter granted by Charles I. Unlike Hawes and Askrigg, it never became industrialised, but it did become a fashionable place to retire to, doubling its population during the early years of Victoria's reign. For some years it boasted a theatre and the Leyburn Shawl Tea Festivals attracted thousands of visitors.

PIC21690   Leyburn Market Place from the church tower in 1889. The church appears to be about six hundred years old, but was in fact only built in 1836; until then Leyburn had no church.

PIC67223   Market day some time in 1914. The building on the left is the Bolton Arms Hotel. A fine Georgian building, the hotel came complete with a Long Room where Leyburn Market Club, founded in 1832, still holds its dinners. In the market place is an iron ring said to date back to days of bull-baiting.

Middleham

Middleham was once a major market town, but it is famous for two things, the training of racehorses and its castle, which was home to no lesser person than Richard III. The original castle was a Norman motte and bailey, the stone keep being added in 1170, followed by a curtain wall and improved living quarters. It eventually passed into the hands of the Neville family and in 1471, Richard, as Duke of Gloucester, came here to be tutored by the Earl of Warwick, whose daughter Anne he later married. Richard's son, Edward, born at Middleham in 1473 also died here in 1484. Anne died soon afterwards and Richard was killed at Bosworth in 1485.

PIC38270   The market place in 1896. Middleham's church of St Alkelda and St Mary, owes its collegiate status to Richard III. Author, Charles Kingsley, was an honorary canon here and once wrote: "This is quite a racing town. Jockeys and grooms crowd the streets. . . ."

Bedale

The market town of Bedale is just a few miles to the north-east of Masham, and three miles from Snape Castle. With its cobbled main street, wide square and bustling market, Bedale sits astride a long, low hill on the edge of Wensleydale.

PIC38283   This picture was taken in 1896 from the tower of St Gregory's Church. In the centre is the old cross, the blur to the left is a pony and trap moving too quickly for the photographer's camera.

PIC38280   St Gregory's Church in 1896. The church was restored in 1854, though the tower itself dates from the fourteenth and fifteenth centuries. There is a room on the first floor, reached by a stair and guarded by a portcullis, which suggests that this was a defensive position for use when the Scots turned up on one of their cattle raids. The Scots are known to have raided at least as far south as Bradford.

Masham

Masham straddles the River Ure on the south eastern edge of Wensleydale, and is the starting off point for excursions to the remains of Jervaulx Abbey. One of Masham's distinctive features is its large market place, where fairs would see as many as 70,000 to 80,000 sheep and lambs up for sale. Masham's claim to fame is that it is the home of Theakstons, brewers since 1827.

PIC60706   Silver Street, Masham in 1908. The Bay Horse Inn was one of several hostelries serving the needs of visitors and locals alike, though the King's Head was said to be the best. The strongest beer brewed by Theakstons is Old Peculiar and is said to be named after the town's ancient ecclesiastical council.

YORK & THE VALE OF YORK
The City of York

The walled city of York was for centuries the second most important city in England. Fortified by the Romans, it was here in AD 306 that Constantine the Great was proclaimed emperor. The historical and cultural capital of northern England, York has managed to survive some, if not all the ravages of time, and is still able to offer visitors a fascinating glimpse into its 2000 years of history. The coming of the railways put York firmly on the tourist map. Though the lines were owned by the North Eastern, no less than five other companies had running powers into the city. The Victorians loved the place, and before the railway came, travellers could get here either by stage or mail-coach and there was a steamboat service to and from London.

PIC63585   Bootham Bar in 1911. Note the overhead wires for the trams. York was a late comer to electric trams, the system not opening until January 1910, and even then it only lasted 25 years.

PIC30632   This is Low Petergate in 1892. On the right is Merriman's pawnbrokers with its ornate gas lamp, whilst on the left is Seale's brush and mat warehouse. Note the large broomhead, which is now in the Castle Museum, hanging over the shop.

PIC30631   An excellent study of shops in Goodrumgate taken in 1892. The opening to the left of Todds leads to College Street and St William's College. The shops to the left were demolished in 1902-3 to make way for Deangate.

PIC30633   Stonegate in 1892. Most of the stone used in the construction of the Minster was carried up this street. The names of streets and alleys are sometimes strange such as Whipmawhopmangate, Jubbergate and so on. One of the more interesting was Mucky Peg's Lane, which unfortunately was changed to Finkle Street.

PIC59785   For decades the first indication for those travelling by train from the south had that York was just a few miles away, was the sight of the lofty towers of the Minster rising majestically above the city. The great central tower is 216 ft high, and the two western towers 202 ft. The picture was taken in 1908.

PIC61723   This is Coney Street in 1909. A fashionable place for shopping, note the liveried coachman and the motorcar. Bicycles appear to be a popular mode of transport for the ladies.

PIC61722   The Shambles in 1909. The shelves at the front of the shops and the hooks overhead, indicate that these were butchers shops.

PIC61702   Lendal Bridge in 1909. Built of cast-iron, the bridge was opened in 1863 and improved the city with direct access to the original railway station which was situated within the city walls.

PIC39492   An 1897 view from the city walls looking towards Lendal Bridge and the towering bulk of the Minster. The road at the right leads to the original railway station, whilst the road cutting under the city wall leads to the new station built in the 1870s.

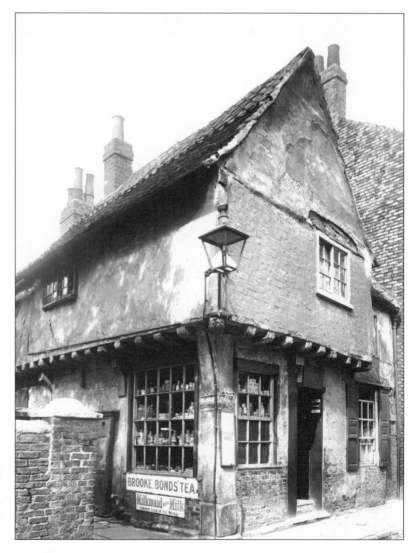

PIC61864   A medieval jettied building with soaring roof and Georgian windows, this old Rectory had been converted into a shop. Street gaslighting was introduced into the city in March 1824, replacing earlier oil lamps.

PIC18494   Barges at York in 1886. For centuries the Ouse had been used to transport people and goods in and out of the city. In the mid-1830s there was even a steamer service linking York with London. The journey took over thirty hours, and was an acceptable alternative to being shaken and bounced along the Great North Road in a mail-coach.

Tadcaster

Just 9 miles from York on the road to Leeds, Tadcaster was once the Roman outpost of Calcaria. Since the eighteenth century, the town has been a centre for the brewing of beer, Samuel Smiths brewery still use water from a well, first commissioned in 1758. Just two miles to the south is the tiny hamlet of Towton, where on 29th March 1461, a bloody battle involving an estimated 50,000 troops took place.

PIC58627   The Market Place and Kirkgate in 1907. The picture was taken from the junction with Bridge Street. Just sneaking in the picture on the right is the recently completed Becketts Bank.

PIC54852   The local breweries used the River Wharfe to bring in raw materials and transport finished products. But the river was prone to flooding with the result that between 1875 and 1877 St Mary's Church was dismantled, moved, and then re-erected out of reach of the waters. In the background is the early eighteenth century Wharfe Bridge.

PIC54849   The viaduct in the background was built in 1849 to carry a railway line, but the line was never built. Tadcaster was however, served by the railway being on the North Eastern's line from Church Fenton to Harrogate.

Selby

An old town on the banks of the navigable Ouse, Selby still sees small motorships loading and unloading at the modest wharf. Shipbuilding was also carried on here, the yard specialising in fishing vessels, small tugboats and inland waterways craft. Because of the width of the river, vessels were launched sideways.

PIC68170   The wooden toll-bridge over the Ouse was built in the eighteenth century. In the background is the abbey church dating from around 1100, the Benedictine monastery to which it belonged being founded in 1069. It is one of the few complete abbey churches, though it has suffered several disasters. At the Dissolution it became the parish church, but in 1690 the south transept was wrecked when the central tower collapsed. In 1906 the abbey was swept by fire, the rebuilding and restoration taking nearly thirty years. This picture was taken in 1918.

PIC65561   Looking down the broad market place towards the abbey. The abbey was founded by Benedict of Auxerre who was instructed in a vision to go to Selebaie in England. Armed with one of the fingers from St Germain, Benedict set off. As he sailed up the Ouse, three swans settled in the water where Selby now stands. Taking this for a sign, Benedict planted a cross, built a hut, and with a lot of help from King William the abbey was founded.

Pictorial Memories Collection

A great new range of publications featuring the work of innovative Victorian photographer Francis Frith.

FRITH PUBLISHING, WATERTON ESTATE, BRIDGEND,
GLAMORGAN, CF31 3XP.

TEL: 01656 668836   FAX: 01656 668710

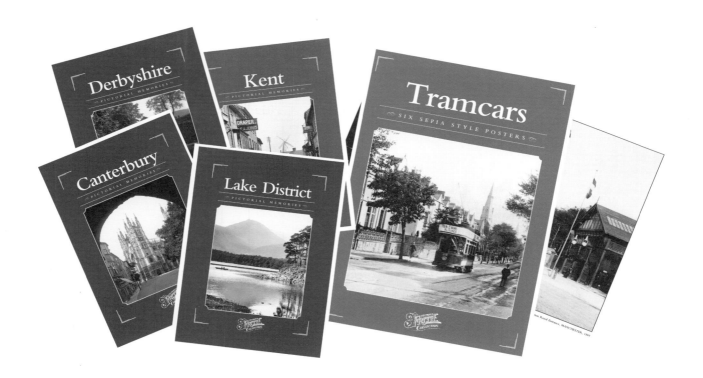

1-84125 *Themed Poster Books* £4.99

000-7	Canals and Waterways	
001-5	High Days and Holidays	
003-1	Lakes and Rivers	
004-x	Piers	
005-8	Railways	
044-9	Ships	
002-3	Stone Circles & Ancient Monuments	
007-4	Tramcars	

Town & City Series £9.99

010-4	Brighton & Hove	
015-5	Canterbury	
012-0	Glasgow & Clydeside	
011-2	Manchester	
040-6	York	

Town & City series Poster Books £5.99

018-x	Around Brighton	
023-6	Canterbury	
043-0	Derby	
020-1	Glasgow	
011-2	Manchester	
041-4	York	

County Series £9.99

024-4	Derbyshire	
028-7	Kent	
029-5	Lake District	
031-7	Leicestershire	
026-0	London	
027-9	Norfolk	
030-9	Sussex	
025-2	Yorkshire	

County Series Poster Books £4.99

032-5	Derbyshire	
036-8	Kent	
037-6	Lake District	
039-2	Leicestershire	
034-1	London	
035-x	Norfolk	
038-4	Sussex	
033-3	Yorkshire	

Available soon

County Series £9.99

045-7	Berkshire	
053-8	Buckinghamshire	
055-4	East Anglia	
077-5	Greater London	
051-1	Lancashire	
047-3	Staffordshire	
049-x	Warwickshire	
063-5	West Yorkshire	

County Series Poster Books £4.99

046-5	Berkshire	
054-6	Buckinghamshire	
056-2	East Anglia	
078-3	Greater London	
052-x	Lancashire	
048-1	Staffordshire	
050-3	Warwickshire	
064-3	West Yorkshire	

Country Series £9.99

075-9	Ireland	
071-6	North Wales	
069-4	South Wales	
073-2	Scotland	

Country Series Poster Books £4.99

076-7	Ireland	
072-4	North Wales	
070-8	South Wales	
074-0	Scotland	

A selection of our 1999 programme:
County Series and Poster Books
Devon, Cornwall, Essex,
Nottinghamshire, Cheshire.

Town and City Series and Poster Books
Bradford, Edinburgh, Liverpool, Nottingham,
Stamford, Bristol, Dublin,
Stratford-upon-Avon, Bath, Lincoln,
Cambridge, Oxford, Matlock, Norwich.

Themed Poster Books
Castles, Fishing, Cricket, Bridges, Cinemas,
The Military, Cars.